11-05-25

F

Snatched By the Devil

By

Jeana Hawkins

## Snatched

When I was thirteen, I thought grownups had a secret world only the initiated and privileged knew. It was the 1970s, the era full of pot smokers and drugs. It was a time when free sex, swingers, nudist colonies and prostitution reigned unbridled; even in the small rural towns of Oklahoma. On this particular day, my father was in a good mood. He took us to the water hole to swim on the Fourth of July. When we got there dad rested on a beach towel, drank wine and waited for his date to show up. A couple of hours later, he was drunk.

I kept walking up and down the bank of the little water hole hoping one of the adults would give me some attention. Finally, a young woman and her date, who were sitting on a grassy slope above the pond, asked me my name and how old I was. "I just turned 13," I said, "It's my birthday, today."

"Where are your parents?" The woman asked.

"My mom's in Tulsa and my dad is over there, waiting on his date."

"He seems preoccupied by his drink," she said.

"Oh yeah, he does that all the time."

"Well, I think it's wrong for him to be getting drunk when he should be paying attention to you, especially on your birthday," said the lady.

"I don't care if he talks to me or not," I lied.

"You have a nice, round little belly.  Do you have a baby in there?" She said.. "Do you know how babies are made?  That's when you have something really nice inside you.  Who's the father?"

I started to cry.  I didn't know if the father was Grandpa or Dad.

An old timer in overalls had overheard our conversation and lumbered over and said, "Why, you look like a caterpillar trying to be a butterfly.  Why, you're just a little girl!"  He seemed nice, but what he said scared me.

The young man with the nice lady said, "I'll kick your dad's ass, if he's the father."

Dad called me and I ran over to him. "Here, help me drink

this wine. My date, I guess, is

not going show up."

The wind picked up and the white fluffy clouds turned black

and gray. God was angry. A big storm came barreling in and

everyone started to clear the park. Lots of commotion was

happening. The young man had spread the word that he thought my

dad had gotten me pregnant and everybody was talking about it. The

old man in overalls did the same. The next thing I knew, the men

went after my dad and threw him on a big hauling truck to go and

beat him, I guess.

My brother got real scared. He had been swimming around

the diving board and hid underneath the dock when all the

commotion started. He stayed there getting waterlogged during the

whole ordeal.

To this day, he's only mentioned it once or twice, and he

panics when he talks about it. He asked me later why I didn't come

and get him. It scared me too, because I couldn't remember why I

didn't. Something terrible must have happened for me not to come

and rescue my little brother whom I loved. But what was it? I would almost remember and then a sense of doom I felt pushed the ordeal deep within my psyche.

Everyone gathered up their families and drove away. The rain began to beat down on my head and shoulders as I stood staring straight ahead. My dad had disappeared. I was still wearing only a swimsuit, and standing alone in the parking lot. The air seemed like a vacuum. That long quiet pause right before something terrible happens–like getting hit by a car. Every sound and move was known. In my mind, my own young, terrible life was passing before me. Memories of being raped by my Grandfather and Dad raced before my eyes. It was just me standing in the once filled, now empty parking lot. It started pouring and the raindrops pounded my head, while I stared straight ahead, not blinking an eye. I could sense someone watching me, a man and woman that I had not seen before. They offered me their umbrella and I took it.

They told me they were there to help me. That the park was being watched by them, a detective and social worker, and they suspected some wrongdoing there. They asked me if I wanted protection from the storm and offered me their car. There was nobody else around to help. I got in the backseat and completely shut down. I said not a word to them. I didn't answer any of their questions. They were beginning to think I was deaf.

The woman said, "She could be in shock."

"We have to act fast. This will tell," he said, reaching over. He burned my knee with his cigar. I screamed. "Well, she's not mute. She's in shock from some kind of trauma."

They watched the sheriff's car drive down the highway in the mist and come into the park. He stopped the car, got out and walked up to the driver's side window. "What are ya'll doing here?"

"We found this little girl without her parents and no way to get home. We thought we would help her."

The sheriff ordered me out of their car and told them the owner and manager of the park wanted everyone to leave. The couple reluctantly drove away and when they were out of sight the sheriff ordered me into his car. My gut instinct knew he was not a nice man. I was about to get snatched by the devil. I started running along the highway.

He ran after me yelling, "Don't run away from me! I have a gun and I'll use it!"

I slipped on the wet grass and fell. I hung onto the barbed wire fence with all my might and he began to pull hard on my leg. He was stretching and turning my leg so much it hurt. I had to let go for fear he would twist my leg out of its socket. He ordered me into the front seat of his police car, and told me to take a sip of his drink.

I knew what that meant. My dad would often ask me to drink bourbon and coke while we were in bed. It was to get me drunk so he could touch me. I knew immediately I was headed for trouble. I could not fight with him. I did as I was told. I took a sip. It had a real bitter taste. He told me he was the sheriff of this area and his last name was McLaughlin. "Have you ever heard of me?"

"No." I asked him to spell it and he did. I knew then, that I wasn't ever going to get away from him, because he didn't mind telling me his name.

He turned off the dispatch to his office and said, "I'm from Arkansas. I managed their juvenile delinquents and got into some trouble there. I came to Oklahoma to do the same thing. The Oklahoma office doesn't know about the trouble and I neglected to give them my social security number." The office here can't track me because of that. Every now and then they ask me to give it to them and I tell them I don't have it memorized. I tell them I'll get it for them and then I don't. So it keeps going back and forth like that. I just say, 'Now you know Arkansas is ass backwards' and the records people just laugh it off."

I said, "But I'm not a juvenile delinquent."

"You're walking down the highway in just a swimsuit. I could tell anybody that asks, you're a prostitute and we can't have that in this area. You see, I used to take care of the delinquents in Arkansas like I am going to take care of you." He sprinkled something into the bourbon and ordered me to drink it. It tasted awful. I felt woozy. That's all I remember until I woke up in a musty, dirt floor basement with a heavy chain on my wrist. The chain was heavy and uncomfortable. I had to hang my arm above my head because the chain was too short to allow me to sit down. I had no clothes on and it was very dark.

I called out into the darkness "Mom!" No answer. "Dad?" Silence. I was hungry. *What did I ever do to my parents to deserve this*? I wondered.

"I'm sorry!" I cried. I tried to piece together how I got there. I couldn't remember.

I fell back to sleep with my right arm shackled above me and kneeling, which was the only position the chain would allow. My joints ached as I crouched on the musty basement floor. Later that night, I heard a noise from upstairs. A lady came down with vegetable soup.

The Sheriff yelled into the darkness at the top of the stairs, "Vegetables for the vegetables. Ha! Ha! Where's the meat? Oh that's ya'll too!" He took another swig of bourbon in the doorway, where we could see him. Then he slammed the door.

I felt hunger pains. The lady gave us the soup and left to go upstairs. I turned to my right and saw two boys, a little one and a teenager like me. The teenager's name was Timmy. They were chained up too. Timmy explained that it's not our fault that we were there. He said the man upstairs was a very bad man.

Timmy and the little boy looked beautiful like two narrow vertical streams of water that were pouring down like a shining waterfall in what little sunlight we had. It's hard to recall what happened exactly, because of the drugs and sleepiness hung over me.

I remember that McLaughlin came downstairs and unchained me. He tossed some clothes at me and told me to put them on. I did.

He said, "I am not telling you to be good. In fact, I want you to be very bad." Then he laughed at his joke. "There is a client upstairs who wants you."

I climbed the stairs as best I could with my skinny, weak legs. I opened the door at the top of the stairs and there sat this man that had burned my knee with his cigar and had told me he was a detective. The Sheriff moved away to give us some privacy with the man sitting at the table by the basement door. I sat beside the man.

He whispered, "Remember me?" I nodded. He acted like he was aroused and was fiddling with the zipper on my pants. "I am trying to bust this guy for kidnapping and child prostitution." I didn't know what he meant but believed that he was there to help me, not hurt me.

The nervous sheriff paced and swirled his drink around while talking to himself. He also saw that nothing much was happening between us. The detective said he is a little hung up when it comes to sex and all he needed was to touch me between my legs while he rubbed himself. He whispered, "I have to pretend that I am molesting you." Sheriff McLaughlin nervously walked back and forth and finally told him to leave.

"Not yet," the detective said, "Don't you want your money?" I whispered for him to get me out of there. He said he couldn't yet. He whispered, "I have to leave you here."

I started to cry. The sheriff thought I was crying because of what he thought the man had done to me. He ordered me to go downstairs. The man left and the sheriff came down and gave me some pills and water. He chained me and then I fell asleep squatting on the floor with my arm dangling above.

I lethargically awakened to an older man with a kind looking face mumbling Bible verses. He was dressed in black with a simple white collar. He crawled on his hands and knees as if he was looking for something. But he wasn't looking for anything. He introduced himself as Godfrey. Apparently he was a preacher and could come and go as he pleased. He was not chained and seemed like a good man. He asked McLaughlin if he could do this as part of some kinky therapy that I didn't understand. He never hurt me or the boys, but then he never helped me escape from the policeman either. One day I asked him why this was happening. He said, "Apostle Paul referred to the devil as wily or crafty." I listened and paused awhile.

I didn't always get to see him and lately I have fallen in and out of sleep while he was there. He was quite comical in a strange weird way crawling around on the dusty floor like a little pig.

I said, "The boys and me are very hungry and weak."

Godfrey said, "You can do all things through Christ who strengthens you when you believe."

"I'm scared...it's like I'm becoming something else instead of a little girl. Who am I now?"

"The Bible says be sober, be vigilant, because your adversary the devil walks about like a roaring lion, seeking whomever he may devour. And we do not wrestle against flesh and blood. Nothing shall be able to separate us from the love of God which is in Christ Jesus our Lord."

I liked talking with him in the darkness and my Baptist upbringing in the church and summer camps helped a little through this difficult time. As a child, prayer was one of my only sources of solace.

Then one day, the sheriff came downstairs and told me to stand up and suck in my tummy. He said if I was lucky, the two men in suit and tie and coming down the stairs would take me to a better place. So I sucked in my stomach as best I could and the sheriff said to the men, "What do you think?"

"I'll pay you $200 for her," one of the men said. McLaughlin unchained me and gave me some fresh clothes. The men took me away, but I don't remember leaving the basement. They must have drugged me again. All I know is I woke up in a room with a large heavy, old looking, wooden door with iron bolts. It looked ominous.

Someone knocked on the door, came in and took me to another room with a bed in it. There was a dark headed woman sitting there by the bed smoking a cigarette. She seemed relaxed like everything was okay. A fat man named John came in and told me to get on the bed and get on my hands and knees. He told me to hold my head up or he will cut my neck with the knife that he held beneath my throat. Then he raped me. It was very painful.

After he raped me, he left the room. I was terrified, and the woman did nothing to help. After she finished her cigarette she left.

I had nothing to defend myself, and thought the terror wasn't over. I moved off the bed and sat in the woman's chair, hoping I could be her, like her, because she didn't get hurt. If I could only get a cigarette, I would really be like her and be safe. That was all the defense I had: my childlike imagination.

But I was wrong. That didn't help me. John came in again and raped me again the same way as before. He told the woman he was trying to kill the spirit in me, so I would do exactly like the men and him told me to do. There was no end in sight for the hell I was going through..

I was taken back to my room by the woman and given what looked like Shepherd's Pie that had been scraped off plates that had already been eaten on. I found out later she was a prostitute and she was to look out for me and follow orders from John at the same time.

She said, "If you want to remember, then eat on the outside of the plate. If you don't want to know what happens, then eat from the center of the plate." I stared at the plate not fully comprehending what she said. It dawned on me later the drugs they put in my food were in the center of the plate. I ate from the outside. It looked like everyone's scraps had been scraped onto my plate. It wasn't much of a meal, but it was something.

The next day I heard they were expecting a big party at this hotel. I got to take a bath in the big metal tub. All the prostitutes were standing around, styling their hair, putting on makeup and trying to figure out what to wear. They were a little happier than I was and seemed to have more freedom than I did. They put makeup on me and gave me something to wear and took me back to my room.

Later that evening, John asked me to sell tickets to the men lined up outside my door. This seemed like freedom to me, so I sold the tickets, but didn't know what the show was that these men in suits and ties came to see that night. Later I was to learn, I was the show.

Being raped by these men one by one, I turned into an animal and started to growl in between the pleas of "No!" as they came through the heavy old door with large nails in it. The drugs wore off and I felt terrible pain in my abdomen because I was too small.

The door opened again and in walked a policeman, detective and paramedic. I was scared. I thought it's going to happen again. I was scared like a wild girl and my straggly hair was in knots. The paramedic came closer to the bed and I robotically leaned backward on the bed with my legs spread open just the way my dad had taught me. I didn't put up a fight. I was tired, too tired to fight anymore.

The paramedic told me to sit up. "It's over" he said, "What's your name?"

I had to think. Nobody had been calling me by my name. I finally said, "Jeana."

"How old are you?"

I paused, "I don't know."

"We're here to help you. We're taking you away from here and getting you some help. Do you know anything else?"

I looked at the desk next to the bed and said, "This is like a hotel, but there is no Gideon Bible in the drawer. I thought every good hotel would have a Bible in the drawer."

I woke up in the Hospital of the county jail alone in a room full of empty beds. There was a guard outside the door. I could not leave.  I was kept there a few days to let the drugs wear off.  I shook violently and sweated.  I was left alone except to eat.  The guard was not supposed to talk to me no matter how bad off I became.  But he finally warmed up to me and said some comforting things.  He had a warmth about him unlike the people feeding me and taking my temperature and cleaning me, but he mostly left me alone.  He did talk to the authorities about me though and the county people didn't want it leaked out what was going on so they switched to a foreign guard who ignored me and also could not understand English.  Whenever I got to go out of the room, I was handcuffed.

Several days later, I quit shaking and throwing up.  They started feeding me a lot to get my weight back to normal.  At first I was paranoid that there were drugs in the food and I refused to eat.  They brought me McDonald's and I threw it up because of the nausea from the pregnancy.  But slowly I trusted them and realized they were trying to help me.

The next thing I remember, I was at a table where some older men were playing cards.  I was feeling well rested, finally.  I think they wondered how I would react socially.  I was no longer handcuffed.  They were cordial, but I don't remember anything else that night.

I was seated in the back of a black car with tinted windows. There were two men in front.  They said they were taking me home. "Do you recognize this neighborhood?  This is home.  Do you know that?  Hey, I have a good joke for you."  He told me the joke but I did not respond by laughing.  I was quiet the whole time.  Numb. When I got out of the car the social worker from the water hole was there and so was the detective.  Mom and my brother were standing together on the front porch..  They did not run over to greet me.  I stood there trying to understand how they hadn't missed me.

My brother asked, "What's wrong with her stomach?"

I felt my stomach and didn't realize how much it protruded.  Mom ignored him and said, "We are doing just fine, my son and I.  I really cannot take on any more responsibility."

The social worker got angry at her and said "If you want to send her away, it would be very detrimental to Jeana.  She needs her home."

I ran to the nice lady and said with all my heart, "I want you to be my mommy!"

She said to me, "You need your family." She turned to my mother, "Well, you've been taking care of her all this time. Has anything changed with you financially speaking that keeps you from taking care of her now? We could get you on welfare, food stamps..."

I don't recall what mom said to the social worker. It hurt too much to know. I looked down. It was obvious mom just did not want me. Her words crushed me. I knew that nothing had changed with her money-wise.

The social worker said to me, "Do you know where your bed is?"

I thought for a moment and said, "Yes."

"Then I want you to go in that house and lie down and get some sleep. You need all the rest you can get," the social worker said in a caring voice, not like my mother's.

I marched up the porch steps and went into my home brushing against mom and my brother who did not reach out to hug me, and I went to my bed and slept for a very long time. Mom told me I slept 20 hours. She never woke me up to try and get me to eat, to get some strength for my skinny body. Nobody did anything to help me digest mentally and emotionally all that had happened. I tried to tell my mother about the strange thoughts and memories in my head and the feelings in my gut.

She said in a mean tone, "I don't want to hear it." And if I cried and kept on talking she'd threaten, "You keep talking like that and I'll ship you off to your dad's."

That terrified me and so I would be quiet. She knew what all my father had done to me because I told her over and over again as I grew up. She threatened me to be quiet anyway. She never held me when I cried. I had to be strong. To this day my mother says the kidnapping never happened. She never faced what I told her.

This memory, which I broke through when I was 25 years old, taught me why I was afraid of barbed wire and police cars and large wooden doors. I always disliked houses built in 1940s with large porch posts and brick around the base. Being caught in heavy rainfall without an umbrella left me crying in the rain.

I learned why I felt different from other teenagers. I became a loner. When I grew up and remembered being kidnapped I saw why I had such low self-esteem and was on the defensive.

At 40, when I cut off my relationship with my mother, I recalled coming home to a distant, cold, angry mother that did not want her pregnant daughter. I could never please her. When I did something wrong she would get angry and hit me and told me I was dumb. This taught me that I never wanted to do anything unless I had good instructions on how to do it right. I feared what my co-workers might do to me if I didn't know how to do my job. I would have anger attacks and sought one specific co-worker to come and rescue me. The co-worker was patient and each time I could see that I didn't have to get angry, anymore when I messed up. I learned to be patient with myself.

After the kidnapping, I feared that Grandma's soup had drugs in it, like the one served in the policeman's basement. The soup had meat and vegetables. After I came home, I felt nauseated and afraid when my mother said, "I love 'meat' and vegetables'."

I recalled these triggers: the barbed wire fences, being caught in the rain, police cars, meat and vegetables and heavy weathered wood doors. They scared me to death, when I saw them in various places as I was growing up. I would have a panic attack and cry. Finally, at 25, I saw why I had these phobias and trained myself to be calm when I encountered them. This helped release the great fear I had deep inside.

I finally mustered the courage to call the Oklahoma police and file a report in 1988. I had remembered the kidnapping within 6 months of the 15 year statute of limitations, since the crime first happened. I was terrified the sheriff would find out and hurt me. The report sat on the District Attorney's desk until the 15 year statute ran out. As far as I know, nothing was done.

For many years after the kidnapping, I couldn't remember coming home. It hurt too much to know. It seemed like I had been in a war and when I came home, nobody wanted me.

## Coming Home

Soon, after coming home I awakened and felt nauseous with a fever. I lay on the bare floor as close as I could against the length of the cold bathtub for several nights. Mom told me I had the flu, but it could have been a pelvic infection from all the sex with those dirty men, or it was morning sickness.

The cramp like feeling and nausea were very painful and sickening. I wondered if I would ever make it. School had started and I couldn't go. Mom wouldn't let me. My stomach got bigger and none of my clothes fit me. I remember going shopping in my night gown because that's all that would fit. She took me to buy full

blouses with an empire waist and jeans for school. She decided I

needed the baby blue jeans with two zippers, one on each hip,

instead of going up the front. I walked to school with both zippers

unzipped and my blouse covered up my big belly.

I don't think I knew I was pregnant. I just thought I was

growing up in different parts of my body. I walked to school. Gym

was my first class with coaches Miss Perry and Miss Dowdy. They

were appalled at how big I was and asked, "Who got you pregnant?"

I couldn't answer. I couldn't tell. I was afraid to talk. I feared I

would break down and cry for days and die, if I told. *Keep it down.*

*Stuff it. Stuff it,* I thought.

The one piece gym suit was tight around my stomach. They

didn't force me to wear a swimsuit. The only shower I got was in

the showers at school. I took the longest to bathe and wished we had

a shower curtain at home. I was tired of taking a bath. Showers got

me cleaner.

I barely remember this part. I don't know how many

months pregnant I was. I think mom took me to get an abortion.

Mom gave me a paper bag to throw up in and another bag full of drugs. I came in and out of consciousness during the abortion. The baby must have gone somewhere. Mom never helped me make sense of it all. The baby blue jeans were too big, now.

Because of the men who forced me to have sex with them, as an adult, I had a fear of intercourse. I would freeze when the lovemaking led to consummation. When I remembered the abuse, I taught myself to relax and enjoy making love. I would not have sex unless I totally trusted my boyfriend. Now I don't have issues with ex. I love sex.

Soon afterward in my Oklahoma history class, I was having emotional turmoil and chattering about the most violent part of my kidnapping. I could not make sense of what was in my mind it was too painful to look at. Mrs. Mulholland, our teacher, said to me, "You are trying to face something very painful and bigger than yourself. To get out of the black hole you are in, you need to rise from the ashes like the Phoenix."

Then she told us the story of the Phoenix. She said, "The Phoenix doesn't just decide to rise again automatically. It is devastated and hopeless. Instead, it gets a small idea, a spark that everything can get better and finally pulls itself up slowly by its own bootstraps."

I said, "How do you do that when you feel a million degrees below nothing."

"With the help of and I'm not supposed to say this in school, but this story is very helpful and important. You can get help from learning about the life of Jesus and that's all I can say legally, since us teachers are not to mention his name in class."

This was the turning point for me. I must have wrapped the little girl within me in a nice warm blanket and tucked her away in my mind, because all the abuse was too much to endure review. It had to be this way since my mother would not allow me to talk about it! So I could not deal with it. I could get good grades, join the drill team and tryout for cheerleading, go to church and try to be a good girl. I did just this and in 9th grade I was nominated along with other girls to be Miss Kittyhawk and Wright Junior High School in Tulsa, Oklahoma.

Aunt Pat

Mom packed up the car and told me to get in. When we got to the dollar store, mom and I went inside. She started looking at the figurines.

"Where are you taking me?  Why can't you answer me? Mommmm, where are we going?  I hope you're not taking me to Dad's. I don't like going to see Dad, Mom  He touches me in places I don't like.  Please?"

All she said was, "I can't help that right now." I started to whimper. I had a sick feeling in my stomach. I was only 14 years old and I had been brave in telling her and she didn't care. I was afraid to tell her this because, what if I pour my heart out and she still takes me to Dad's. That would really hurt. It would be just like all the other times, and then I would know for sure that she didn't love me.

"Why don't you go look around the store?" she said.

So, I did. I always did as she told me. I went to the next isle and a lady came over and whispered to me, "I heard what happened and believe me, you made yourself clear. I wouldn't give her anymore regard and it's alright not to love her. Believe me, she will get hers." That helped a little but I just cried all the way to the checkout stand.

There were several cashier's running totals on half a dozen women of all shapes, colors and ages. One of the cashiers asked me what was wrong. "You're one of our customers too and we care about you. What happened?" I bawled. I looked at mom and she turned her nose up at the whole ordeal.

Finally I choked out, "Mom is taking me to stay with my father and I don't want to go. He touches me and does things to me that I don't like. He tries to get me to do things I don't want to do."

One of the women said, "I know exactly how you feel. My mother did the same thing. She ignored my cries for help."

"Swept it under the rug," said another lady.

Mom said, "There isn't anything I can do about it. "

"I'm with you. You can't do anything", one of the ladies said.

The other ladies jumped on her. "You could call the police!"

"You could shoot the man!"

"Yeah!" several yelled. Some women started yelling at Mom and some started yelling at each other. One mother said to her daughter, "You do that with him just to spite me!"

One young lady in tears said, "I never told anyone. I thought it only happened to me."

Others were crying. "This is the reason I am so overweight! I eat to get rid of my awful feelings about being molested."

"Raped," said another.  The women were yelling and crying and mom just wanted to get away from the fiasco.

As we were leaving, one lady said, "This is why I hate sex and I'm married."

"Do something about it, bitch!" a lady yelled at Mom.

Mom made me leave with her but I wanted to stay with the ladies.  They were real and felt like me and were actually talking about it.  But Mom didn't care.  I knew where we were headed now that we were in the car.  I knew what was going to happen.  My eyes glazed over and my hand released the empty Coke can.  It fell to the car mat.  *If she wouldn't protect me, then I would the only way I knew how*, I thought.  I zoned out.

She looked at her lipstick in the mirror and adjusted her hair and then started the car just as usual.  She drove until she got to the truck stop and left me with Dad and his sister, Pat.  The conversation was boring so I got up from the booth and looked around.  It was as if all that commotion at the dollar store hadn't happened.  Pat got up from the table to find me and I guess, check on me.  She found me.  I was in the gift shop of the truck stop.  I was looking at the childlike porcelain angels that had the days of the week on little hearts.  Pat and I picked out Wednesday's angel and she bought it for me. She said she thought she knew how I felt. She said it made me feel like nobody wanted me. If I didn't already know it, I knew it then. I told her I didn't like Dad and Mom and I felt worthless.

"I know and I will tell your dad to leave you alone at night and you must stay in your own bed. His behavior must stop." A tear came down my cheek. "Why don't you come home and stay with me," she said.

I cried some more. The last thing I wanted was to stay with my Aunt Pat. Then I would have to admit that both my mom and dad hated me. She was a spinster. She lived outside of a tiny town in Oklahoma. Her house was homely with chickens scratching at the dirt in the backyard and flea ridden dogs lying on the front porch.

Aunt Pat, Dad and I went to see my Dad's brother and eleven children in a rickety house in Bekoshe, Oklahoma. For a while the women chatted round the kitchen table.

Incest was brought up and they all agreed, "There is absolutely nothing that can be done about it."

I said, "Well, we could get a gun!" They gasped.

Aunt Pat said in a reverent tone, "Haven't you ever heard of 'thou shalt not kill?"

Another said, "I get through it by my faith."

I asked, "So it makes you feel bad and hurts you like it does me?"

She said, "Yes."

I said, "You know the men don't feel bad. They do exactly what they want and go on with their lives."

Dad took me home. That night I got dressed for bed in my room in the trailer. I hoped to rest the whole night through in MY bed, instead of his. I turned out the light and sat on the bed. He walked in and said, "You ready for bed?"

"Yeah." He sat down on the bed and put his arms around me. I fell asleep to numb myself. He thought my ability to fall asleep so easily was because I felt comfortable. But really, I became dormant because I was afraid. He didn't know it but over the years of abuse, I was not able to evade him physically, but could escape him mentally by my ability to fall asleep at my own command. It was the only defense I had against him.

In the morning, I awoke prepared to remember what wrongdoing was done to me. I discovered that nothing had happened. Dad must have been trying to turn over a new leaf. How long would it last?

I refused to move in with Pat, so I was sent back to Mom's.

## PART TWO

### Small Town Girl

I was born in Keota, Oklahoma  Keota was a small town. It was no more than a stone's throw. Hardly anybody stayed in the jail overnight, since Great Grandpa Greenwalt came into town to shoot the sheriff with his pearl handled gun.

It seems that some Greenwalts, had crossed some Indian territory to go hunting. They thought it would be okay since they didn't tamper with anything. The Indians warned them year after year. One night the Indians came onto Greenwalt property. They found the stables which held horses and combines (concubines, my father had nicknamed them). My dad said once, "Some farmers have combines, some have concubines. The Greenwalts have both."

The stables, made of old weathered wood, lit up the night with explosions into smithereens from the combine fuel igniting and startled the horses. The horses made it out safely, but the barn and combines were scorched and ruined. Great Grandpa Greenwalt rode into town to talk to the lazy sheriff who wouldn't do anything. He shot the lazy sheriff in the arm. All kinds of wrongdoing were done in this town and nobody talked about it because they were either a Christian, guilty or both. Many decades later Keota was still a small town. I was four years old. The sheriff's office is a convenience store, gas station and a one room jail that houses a cot with no door or lock. Late at night the jail bird might get hungry, so he could pick up candy, lift leftover hot dogs and grab a six pack from up front. He would deny it the next day, so he wouldn't have to pay. I know because my dad stayed there a while for stalking mom even after she had gotten a restraining order on him.

They weren't divorced, but mom had left him on numerous occasions and took my little brother, leaving me with my alcoholic pedophile father. He always had to have his hands where they didn't belong and beer wasn't his only vice. Mom didn't care when I cried. She left me there anyhow to sleep with my dad on the small flimsy cot. The next morning, Mom stopped by to get a tank of gas. When she got ready to leave, the sheriff was ringing up the charges for my mom to pay, "Okay, two tanks of gas, two packs of cigarettes, a six pack, two candy bars, one hot dog, chips, four Cokes. That's 30 dollars and thirty-five cents," he said.

"What?" my mom said, "If you think I'm going to pay for that bastard, you've got another thing coming."

"But he doesn't have a job, so he has no money and somebody's got to pay."

"Well, I don't have the money either and I am late for work!" She was a secretary at an accounting firm.

"Oh, so YOU have a job, so YOU can pay. That will be fifty dollars and thirty-five cents!"

I started crying. My brother started crying.. Mom started yelling. There was a long line of customers impatiently waiting their turn and they started yelling too. The sheriff thought he just couldn't take it anymore. He had to get paid. Finally, I don't know if mom paid him or not, but she left me with my dad.

There were two churches, Baptist and Episcopalian, down the hill from Main Street. The Baptists felt good about themselves because the minister preached the meek will inherit the Earth and money is the root of all evil. The Episcopalian church believed that it's good to have money in order to do good works with it. The Baptists thought they were sinners.

There was also no library. I guess for some the Bible was the only book they felt they needed. Beer was also the other local religion. They drank especially at the smoke filled pool hall. My parents liked beer and drugs.

The Plastic Pillow

I was in my early forties before I remembered the incident.

It took me that long to be brave enough and ready enough to let my consciousness know about the day she left. When I was four years old, mom put a restraining order on my father and got a separation from him. Soon afterwards, one early morning Mother hid my three year old little brother Richard behind the rack of clothes that were hung in the back seat of her car. I came out of the house running as fast as my little legs would go. I could see my brother's small feet peeking out from behind the clothes rack.

"Take me, Mom!" I yelled.

For days they had been moving out of the house in Keota. But I knew this was the last trip out the door with their stuff.

"No, Jeana, you're not going with us!" Mother said sternly.

My brother stuck his head out of the clothes and said, "Mommy, I had a bad dream."

I thought, *that's funny, why is Richard in the back seat? That's where I go.*

"No!" Mom yelled and chased me around the car. "You are not coming with us!" I managed to get in the front seat of the car.

Richard repeated, "Mommy, I had a bad dream." He cried.

"Well honey what is it?" she said with concern in a syrupy voice.

"I had a bad dream too." I said.

"Shut up!" Mom snapped at me. "I will not allow your filthy mind to rub off on him! You'll ruin him. Get out of the car now!" Afraid of her, I scrambled out of the car. I always did as I was told, for fear she would hit me if I didn't.

"Go up the steps and go inside," she commanded. Mom followed me up the stairs to take one more look to see if anything had been left behind. She saw an old plastic pillow she had found on the side of the road. She decided to take it with her. That was the lowest point for me. She would rather take the dirty lost pillow than take me. Then she locked me inside the empty house.

I watched my Mom check her lipstick and eye makeup in the rear view mirror then start the car. She pulled out of the driveway and drove down the gravel road. I heard later that she headed off to Mississippi with my brother to see her sister. There was only one piece of furniture in the house. I was my bed and I crawled into it. My heart was broken in two. My brother got to go and I was left behind. Was something wrong with me that my mother continually favored Richard over me? For days I lay there, hungry and very thirsty. But the cabinets and the refrigerator were empty. I was thirsty but the faucet was too high. I didn't think of using the bathtub faucet. The water was probably turned off, anyway. I felt very alone. The only telephone was mounted high on the wall and there was no chair to reach it. I cried and tried to sleep instead of feeling all these emotions that were spinning in circles above me.

Mom had left Dad on numerous occasions. This last time she left me locked up inside the house alone. As I lay in my bed in the otherwise empty place, I tried not to think of things that would make me cry. I wanted to die so I wouldn't feel the sorrow and pain in my heart. My stomach churned with sadness that was so painful it swirled above me. Then I thought of Mertie, my babysitter.

Mertie, the next door neighbor would babysit me, so mom would have exclusive time to play with my little brother, Richard. Mertie taught me my colors and let me color in the Sears Catalog. I would mark through the models toothy grins with a crayon and say, "Mommy, no smile."

Then I remembered Mommy, Richard and I playing in the yard and I showed Mommy a big smile and got none in return. She ignored me and started playing with my brother on the scooter.

Mertie saw this and chimed in and called to me and I came running and smiling at her. She put her hand to my face and said "God! When your eyes light up and when you smile you are showing God within you."

"God?"

"Yes. God created everything. God is love and you have God inside you." This made me very happy. I didn't exactly know what she was saying but I knew it was super good about me.

Mertie was married to Conn and they went to AA meetings for many years. All their children were grown so Richard and I meant a great deal to them. But mom caught on that Mertie knew she drank beer every day, even when she first woke up. Mom and Dad moved less than a mile away in the little town and started taking me to different babysitters. They were mentally challenged or couldn't speak English. All because there was no telling what horrendous things would come out of my mouth: like how my dad molested me and how my mother didn't like me. Dad hit Mom and Mom hit me. I don't know what all happened to my brother, but I think he didn't get by so easily, either. He was bullied by my dad and smothered by my mother. I taught him his ABCs.

Before today, the day my mother left me, Mertie had walked across town, about one mile to our new house. She had found me alone in the house while mom and dad were at work and Richard was being babysat by Mrs. Kemp.

Mertie tried to explain to me why she couldn't babysit me anymore. My parents didn't want a good lady to babysit me, because she asked my parents too many questions about my upbringing. We both cried. She decided to leave before mom got home, because who knows what my parents would have done if they knew she was there talking to me. Mertie had brought a teacup in her purse and took it out carefully and put it on the dinner table for me to see. She said, "I drink tea. Your parents drink beer. I'm leaving this teacup for you to remember me by." I remember the teacup. It was cream colored and had tiny copper *fleur de lis* all over it. It was beautiful. Mertie left and that's the last time I saw her. I cherished that teacup and saucer.

Mom saw the cup Mertie had left for me and became angry. It disappeared shortly after. Many years later, I would ask my mother why she wouldn't take me to Mertie's anymore. She said, "Because it was inconvenient." That was a lie. It was less than a mile away.  Mertie would have walked there to babysit me for free.

It was difficult at first to figure all this out but when I was older,  I

eventually figure out the truth. Knowing Mertie made me strong.

Mertie always knew what to do.  Mertie always knew what to say.

I don't know how many days and nights I lay in my bed, but

Mom's mother, my Grandma, came to the house, curious about

whether mom left anything when she went to Mississippi with

Richard.  She thought, they'd moved so there wouldn't be anything

inside; but something told her to go anyhow.  When she let herself in

with her key, she was shocked to see me.  It had been several days

since my mother had left.  I lay in bed in a deep sleep.  She tried to

wake me and I tried to see and hear her despite the great fog and

weakness that hung over me.

"Grandma?" I murmured trying to lift my head.

"Yes, it's me.  I'm going to get your Grandpa in here and he

will carry you to the truck.  We'll go home and get you something to

eat and get you all cleaned up."

I tried to cry happy tears, but all I could say in a raspy

voice, "Mommy gone!"  My mouth was parched.  I thought,

*Grandma's not Mertie, but she is a good lady too.*  Grandma took me home and bathed me. I cried because I knew I was being loved and she cried because she knew I knew it. After the bath, Grandma heated up some homemade soup made from vegetables in her garden. At first I only drank the broth because I was so thirsty. Then I got my appetite.

I lived with Grandma and Grandpa and went shopping for first grade school supplies with them. At the checkout corner a 4 foot tall stuffed rabbit stood on its hind legs like a man.

"I need this rabbit to keep Dad away," I said to the clerk. So he'll beat dad up for putting his awful thing in my mouth!"

"If that's what's wrong, then you need to call the police," she said.

"Oh, she doesn't see him much anymore," Her Grandma said. "Her parents are getting a divorce."

"But if he gets partial custody, he can still do her harm."

"Now you be quiet. You're embarrassing us!" Grandma scolded me.

The clerk and I realized they were not going to do anything about it. I wailed. Sometimes kids scream and cry in grocery stores for a good reason. Grandma put the rabbit back and the clerk was furious at that and said, "The least you could do is buy her the rabbit! He's her only ally." She had tears in her eyes as she watched me go.

They were churchgoers and did not talk about sexual abuse in public, because they were good Christians. I got a good whipping once we were out of the store. Yes, they were good Christians. They taught me dancing was wrong. They didn't even like square dancing. Never say God's name in vain. They told Richard and I not to believe precious gems had meaning as some believe in their new age beliefs. No swearing. They were Baptists.

Not only that, but Grandpa wouldn't teach Grandma how to drive. One time Grandma suspected Grandpa of having an affair. He drove into town several miles on his ancient tractor with his sickle to mow the widow's yard. Grandma thought he had been gone far too long, so there must be something going on that she wasn't supposed to know about. She loaded me into the truck and took off. She didn't know how to drive and went past the widow's house looking for Grandpa's tractor. She was doing some major league swerving back and forth on the old dirt road, down into the ditches and back on the road. I don't remember anything else after that. Maybe Grandma crashed in the ditch which I hurt my head. She never talked about it after that.

Also, there was no drinking allowed. Grandpa wouldn't let her or let any of their grown children drink when they came to visit, but the mail carrier always put a bottle of bourbon in his mailbox. He forbade Grandma to get the mail, so she wouldn't know about his secret stash. But one time when my brother came for a visit, we found it when we were playing. First thing we did was tell Grandpa what we had found. He acted surprised. My brother and Grandpa and I went to the mailbox together and Grandpa took out the bottle. He opened it up and said we could taste it as long as we didn't tell Grandma. He held it up to my nose and "Whew!" it smelled horrible. I didn't take a drink and neither did my brother. But my Grandpa did and then I hated the way he started to look at me. Then Grandpa swatted us once on the butt. He told us, "The mailbox was his property and we had no business getting in it and Grandma doesn't know about it." Grandma and Grandpa abided by these rules. I thought they loved me in their own way. They were Christians by day, but by night Grandpa was a very mean pedophile like my dad.

Later on when I was 11, Grandma told me she can't do anything about the incest and she knew about my dad hurting me and mom not doing anything about it. That's one reason she kept a secret bottle of liquor that she stole from the mailbox when Grandpa wasn't looking. She hid it between the side of their house and the tree trunk by the back door. She had a candy dish inside by the door full of candied orange slices for bad breath so nobody could tell when she drank.

One time I remember Grandpa asking me where Grandma was. "Oh she must be in the garden," I said.

I wasn't supposed to tell when Grandma was on the back porch drinking and sometimes smoking. He took this opportunity to hurt me in a sexual way. He could make me feel degraded and filthy and worthless. He went back to the shed and I found Grandma on the back porch. I had tears of anger in my eyes and this time she told me to drink it and I did, but she wouldn't let me have a cigarette. We got drunk to kill the pain, but she wouldn't let me smoke a cigarette because "That," she said, "wouldn't help me in this situation."

I think this closet drinking runs in this tightknit family.  I have a cousin that empties the olive jar of its juice leaving the olives and pours vodka into it so his wife won't know he is getting drunk.  During commercials he would go to the refrigerator and take a secret swig.  Patty, his wife, didn't know because she hated olives!

The Kitchen Ladies

One day, when I was old enough to walk home from school, I didn't. Mom had a drunken tirade the night before, and I was afraid she would be mean to me some more, when I got home from school. So, I fell asleep and stayed all night in the bushes at school. The janitor found me the next day with my hair in disarray and knotted with dirt.

Mom hardly ever made me breakfast and dinner. In the morning, I would get out of the car and linger by the school kitchen on my way to my first class, smelling the great aromas coming out of the door. The lunch ladies would sneak me an individual size milk and sometimes a cinnamon roll. I especially liked the kitchen ladies leftover chocolate pudding from lunch the day before. It would sit outside the refrigerator and get a thick rich chocolate skin on it. I liked to scoop the soft pudding from underneath and eat that first. When that was gone I would eat the best part, the hardened fudge-like layer on top. Yay!

I remember the beginning of my fifth grade year. All us kids were in the first line to go to lunch and I was feeling funny–very weak. A teacher asked us if there were any of us who were real hungry. If they were, the kids would go to the front of the line and get their tray of food first. All of a sudden, I felt weak and shaky. I fell to the floor and passed out. They revived me and sent me to the front of the line. I couldn't tell anybody what I was feeling and could not lift and hold my tray. I couldn't hardly stand up and bounced my body onto the wall, so that the wall could kind of hold me up. Finally, they saw how weak I was and carried my tray. They picked out my lunch, because I couldn't do it myself. I don't remember eating, but I must have been spoon fed like a baby. Very often, school lunches were my only meal. It was horrible in the summers, because Mom didn't cook much or very well. She was proud that she didn't cook. She pretended she was a rich lady that had cooks and maids.

## College Girl

Mom was still hardly ever at home. I did feel that the image of God was inside me, a part of my being like Mertie said, but I still kept the abuse pushed down below my level of consciousness. My senior year in high school proved to be more promising. I heard there was money to be given away to students wanting to go to college. There were scholarships, grants, loans, and non-academic financial aid. My school counselor confirmed this. So I made regular trips to my neighborhood library to research this in the very thick catalog of Barron's Guide to Colleges. I started with A for Alabama and read until I came to the V's for Virginia. I was looking for a school that gave away a large percentage of grants and financial aid. A college in Virginia caught my interest. They had a liberal arts program and a high percentage of gifts of aid to financially needy students.

Just as I finished reading about it, the librarian came into the room and asked me how I was doing. Her name was Mrs.Carlson and she said her daughter went there and she knew a prominent alumna in town that could help me.

I was so excited! What a coincidence! It was meant to be! I was so sure I could get the funds and be accepted that I only filled out one application to that college. One day early in the summer after my senior year in high school I opened the mailbox. There was a letter from the college of my choice! I opened it and read the acceptance letter and financial aid package.

I was so happy. I told Mom when she came home from work. She was not thrilled and told me I would never make it. But I knew I could. Meals were included in the package and I could work during the summer to get spending money. I also had a car that my Father had bought me and I could buy the gasoline and drive there. I got two jobs in the summer and worked part time at college.

My life began to change for the better. The women's college was tucked away in the hills of Virginia. I left for Virginia and was finally free of my bad high school reputation and started to date some nice young men.

My first year, my mom's millionaire boyfriend, Charlie, paid for me to ride horses English style at an equestrian ranch. I made good friends with the other girls who were taking lessons. The girls in the class knew I needed a riding habit and helped me by giving me some of their clothes to wear in the shows: jodhpurs, a blouse, collar and jacket. I didn't have money for black leather riding boots. I took 1st place in a show and got a blue ribbon and silver candy tray for winning.

Even though mom was dating Charlie she rarely asked him for money to help me out. She also didn't want me to have contact with him by mail or phone and not to even send a thank you card. I always did as mom told me. I found out later there was a pattern of this with her other well off boyfriends. She was afraid I would take them away from her in a sexual way like she thought I did her husband when I was only a little girl.

I needed braces, glasses, clothes, psychological help and spending money and allergy medicine. I received none of these. I had to buy black rubber rain boots to wear with my riding habit during shows. They looked awful.

Charlie had told me during the summer before going to college he would give me $500.00 a semester, if I would quit working one of my jobs. I had been working since I was thirteen. He said he wanted me to have fun. He gave the money to Mom and she kept it to spend on clothes for herself, cocaine and liquor. I was very sad about not being like the other girls.

I have to say as I write this that it's very difficult to forgive her. When you have access to money like she did, I think it's abusive to not help your own child.

It is like what the French Canadians say, "Je me souviens," which translates to "We forgive, but not forget." To me if I could forgive I wouldn't have angry thoughts about her everyday. Lately, I have been saying this phrase and it helps.

I joined clubs like the Fine Arts Committee and we went to New York City to see the sights and a Broadway Show. My advertising class also went to Madison Avenue of NYC to get the inside scoop on how to get a job there and learn techniques in advertising. During my junior year I spent a month at the New York Stock Exchange and worked the whole summer at the American Stock Exchange. This was made possible because of Charlie. It was an exciting time in my life and provided some of my fondest memories.

I did not exactly fit into the stereotype of the girls at my college, but I found my niche. I see now that it taught me what I wasn't. It taught me what I didn't know. It may seem superficial, but I didn't have the money to buy the L.L. Bean moccasins, the Tartan plaid kilt and Fair Isle sweater with a matching Skyr turtleneck and gold add-a-bead necklace they all wore. I wanted to be just like the young ladies at this school.

My senior year in college was tough. I came back to school in Virginia from Wall Street to finish the final year for my B.A. degree. It was a depressing year. Mom and her boyfriend split up after 4 years. This meant I lost my contact in NYC and Wall Street.

I went home school after my senior year was over with my tail between my legs hoping for and stock brokerage job. I finally landed a job at E.F. Hutton.

While at E.F. Hutton, I saved money to go backpacking in Europe. I only made $15,000.00 a year. To save money, I stayed at home on weekends and taught myself to cook instead of going out to bars with my girlfriends. I hardly ever drank alcohol. I also brought my lunch to work and parked in the furthest parking lot I could away from work. I did this because the lot across from work cost $5.00 a day and my lot was 25 cents a day. Even in the snow and cold weather, I would walk in my heels to work, knowing that for every two days I did this I would have $10.00 to spend in Greece and could live like a queen on the beach. It was 1985 and the dollar was super strong compared to the Euro dollar and so I knew I would have a blast!

I was walking down a semi-residential somewhat commercial street in Paris. An American woman in a car slowed and rolled down the window. She said, "Be careful! Men from the Middle East are kidnapping girls and abuse them and take them to their homeland. Its called sex trafficking. I think they are following you!"

"Oh," I said, "I will be careful, thank you."

The car drove off. I looked behind me. Nobody was there. Suddenly I felt a black scary cloud get into my mind. I had racing thoughts. I felt fear and anger. The buried memories of my kidnapping when I was thirteen came to mind and then I couldn't see. I kept walking, now, with my hands out in front of me. "Help!" I said. I slowly came out of the brain fog and could see a man in his 50s sitting on a park bench. He told me he was a doctor and was glad he came out here for his break. "Something told me to," he said, "Sometimes, mental stress can be so great that your vision can go away, temporarily. What were you thinking about?"

"It was black, dark a scary place. I thought about my mother and there were men."

"Are you travelling? Are you alone?"

"Yes I'm on vacation and right now I'm alone."

"Then you don't want to think about that right now. Try to collect yourself and finish you trip." His words helped ground me. After a little while he said, "Well I have to be getting back to my job. I have an appointment soon." He left me on the bench alone and I collected myself and got up and continued my walk.

One thing I learned while in Europe was that if I didn't like the people I was traveling with, all I had to do was change the scenery: get on a train and go somewhere else and make new friends, instead of accepting other people's views of me. I didn't have to change them and they didn't have to change me. The family I grew up with tried to put me in a position of a stupid scapegoat. Now know I don't have to accept that.

Back home, I changed jobs often, searching for a better paying one. I stayed in the stock brokerage business. Sometimes my past would lurch out at me if I was caught in the rain without an umbrella or if I walked near a barbed wire fence out in the country. But the egg shell still did not crack open and spill all the memories so I could see clearly. Memories continually tried to hatch but only made a small crack in my shell. My past did not come fully forward until I was financially able to pay for a therapist. Then and only then was I ready to fall into the abyss of my mind.

## Remembering

I was twenty-five and driving with a friend and co-worker near my apartment in Huntington Beach, California. A commercial about a local dentist came on the radio. After the commercial I remarked, "I need braces for my crooked teeth." Bill said, "Has anybody hit you to make them crooked?"

"I don't think so," I said. I didn't think what he said was funny. He explained that for fun he and another friend would ask people, "Has anybody ever hit you?" I didn't think that was humorous at all.

After a pause, he said, "My father use to slap me. But the last time he ever hit me, all my family were together at the dinner table. I'd made a snide remark about my mother's cooking. My dad yelled, 'Don't ever talk to your mother that way'. My dad raised up his hand to slap me in the face and I caught his arm and said, 'That's the last time you will ever hit or slap me! Don't do that again! I admit I shouldn't have said that about mom's cooking but you shouldn't hit me over it.' He added, "Has anything like that happened to you?"

I said, "No, I don't think so. I'm not sure."

The next day, I was driving home after work. I thought about the conversation I had with Bill. Then I had a sudden flashback: my mother had slapped me in the mouth over and over again. She knocked me to the ground and then I couldn't remember anything else, except that she was holding a bottle of beer. I was only 4 years old. It was very real, not surreal. I felt the surprise and pain all over again.

I started to cry. Then I got angry. I need therapy, I thought. But I didn't think I made enough money to see a therapist. I concentrated on my driving. I spotted a bookstore and had a sudden thought. I had a feeling there were many more memories that hadn't surfaced.

I pulled into the bookstore's parking lot and went inside the shop. I told the clerk what had happened and got tears in my eyes. "Where's the psychology section," I asked.

He took me over to it. "If I was in your shoes I would read a book on dysfunctional families. Does your mother drink?"

I said, "I don't know. Does it matter?"

"Yes it does. You might get a lot out of this book, <u>Healing The Child Within: Discovery and Recovery for Adult Children of Dysfunctional Families,</u> by Charles L. Whitfield, M.D."

I looked at the book and the picture of him on the back of the book. There was something very nice about him. His eyes looked soothing and intelligent.

I bought the book and immediately went home and read it all in two days. The book pushed my buttons. It made me cry and get angry. One memory in particular that came up was prom night in my senior year of high school. Mom had told me I couldn't go to the prom, because she didn't have the money for my dress. But I began looking for a dress anyway. Somehow mom got the money, probably from her married millionaire boyfriend. I got my hair done at the beauty salon. My date was Mike, a friend of mine. I was so proud.

After the prom Mike and some friends stopped by my house to get some gift baskets filled with cheese, crackers and wine. I picked one up and it was unwrapped. A bottle of wine fell to the floor and broke open. I cursed and then said, "The carpet is wet."

Mom walked into the room in a see-through gown and said to Mike, "I'm wet too." They got real close to each other and started kissing and making out. I stared in shock. *"How could she do this?"* I thought. I waited for them to stop.

My friends and their dates were in the car waiting for Mike and I to come out with the baskets. Matt got tired of waiting and came to the door. He saw what was going on and glanced at me staring in shock. He grabbed me and took me to the car. He took us to their fraternity house. I remember my friends waiting for me to say something. I pretended to be in a good mood. I had already blocked it out. My friends were trying to get me to talk about it. They wanted to know my feelings. I remember them saying Maria has a date here. And so does DeAnn and Beth. Where's your date? Do you remember?

I said, "What are ya'll talking about? Why are you asking me all these questions?" Mike finally arrived an hour later and went to bed with no apology and had nothing to say to me. I had nothing to say to him.

When I finished <u>Healing the Child Within</u>, I went to work and a feeling came over me. I felt I was looking at the world in a whole new way. Like a fresh day after a big rain or big cry. I felt strong. I could take on anything that came my way because I had the tools now to deal with obstacles and opportunities. The book gave my mind the tools it needed to help me remember and to know right from wrong. So in January 1987 and at 25 years old, it was time to make a serious New Year's Resolution. My resolution was to take on whatever big event that was going to happen. I decided to remain open. Something bigger than I knew was going on here.

Memories flooded into my mind. It was like I had a double life and I was just then finding out about it. Before the book, I would see scant images in the recesses of my mind and feel awful feelings, but could not make sense of them to bring it to my consciousness. After reading this book, I could finally remember the abuse because when it came to mind, I could say, "That was wrong to have happened. That hurt me. That wasn't right." I was parenting myself. I realized that Mom swept much of my problems under the rug and now I could look in the darkness beneath and bring them to light.

At first, I felt the revulsion others might have, if they ever found out about my secrets and skeletons in my closet. I felt alienated from my friends and co-workers. But the feelings I felt about myself was pure love. I had more love for myself than I had ever known before, because I remembered the little child within that I saw for the very first time. Because of this I likened myself to a small rose bud about to grow into a rose through my strength within and my hope. It still took many years to admit that I had been kidnapped, because of the horrific memories. I would say, "She (my child within) was kidnapped. It happened to her."

When you see your abused inner child is intrinsically good, you know that from that day forward, it is part of your conscious personality. This is going to make you into a better person, because that part of you has been missing all this time.

When I first remembered at 25 years old, I was very angry for weeks. Then one night, I caught a glimpse of that little girl and my heart melted. I was no longer angry. Instead I ached for her. I felt her sadness and pain. My little girl was smart back then. She was pretty with big brown eyes and long brown hair. She knew all things. She was precious. I saw the movie, E.T. and felt my little girl was like him: funny, good, sweet, abandoned and alienated.. She was a light shining in the darkness, when her family left her.

When I fully clarified the abuse through therapy, I knew I still had to hold down my job. How was I going to work when this abominable problem was on my mind? I thought I couldn't let her out of my mind. She's hurting and I have to help.

Then I thought about Lou Benzel, my next door neighbor when I was in 7th grade. She told me she had a feeling that I was like the man, Job, in the Bible. That I would go through many trials and tribulations like he did. At first he questioned God and then after all these hardships, he came to need and believe in Him and His Son. So also, I thought about how can I. Then I remembered her telling me that Jesus watches over your burdens so you can lead your life. I imagined Jesus in my mind and thought about how I was placing my mistreated little girl in his arms to lovingly watch over her and her burdens, just how I would have watched over her one day at a time.

For problems of this magnitude you have to bring out the big guns, one day at a time with His love. Alcoholics Anonymous call it turning it over to your Higher Power. The problem seemed insurmountable. So I just lived one day at a time and kept turning it over to God so I could work. When I came home from work, I would take her back and grieve for her, then give her back to Jesus the next day when I went back to work. I had no family in California. They were in Texas.

In the Bible, 1 John 1:4-5, it says, "*The Word was the source of life, and this life brought light to mankind. The light shines in the darkness and the darkness has never put it out.*" I started having memories of my father sexually abusing me. I found this to be disgusting and could barely come to grips with it. Soon afterward, my thoughts took a sharp turn and I started remembering the kidnapping. This was easier to think about than what my Dad and Mother had done. I realized that I had a light in myself even in the basement long ago where I buried it. The light was hidden inside me and almost burnt out. My little girl had been forgotten about. Every now and then in my life she would come out and show her horror and scare the daylights out of me. But now I could see my experiences would define and refine my character according to God's plan.

I believe you get poise and maturity when you finally understand and accept yourself and your past. In Florence Littauer's book, Freeing the Mind from Ties that Bind, "God will use all our experiences to His honor and glory, and we will feel uplifted and valued!" I used to feel betrayed by God for allowing these horrible things to happen to me. Now I can see that my experiences are a way to keep me close to Him and help others by telling my story. I came to know him better, the more I came to understand myself. We are born in God within a capsule. It disappears and reappears later in life unscathed. I must polish it to let it shine.

Soon after reading The Child Within, when I was 25, I went home to Texas from California to visit Mom. I told her Dad raped me. She said, "Sounds like something he would do." That hurt immensely because in that moment I knew she knew back then and didn't protect me. I had been wanting a apology, and never got one.

I write with my non-dominant hand. The non-dominant hand signifies the inner child and the other dominant hand is the adult. Writing this way in a journal will surprise you with information about how your inner child feels and thinks.

'I am mad at mom. I don't want a relationship with her. Don't call her. Don't email her and don't send thank-you cards for gifts she sends to me,' my non-dominant hand wrote.

'Okay, it will hurt her but I know you are in more pain. She made me feel second best to my brother, but there is more. If my little girl writes more at night, then I will be more efficient during the day and use my time wisely. At night, I can take her to her special place. I need to tell my case manager that I don't want a relationship with mom,' my parent hand wrote.

'Mom had done enough damage. I told everybody and nobody helped. I don't want anybody, anymore! She trashed me! She did not protect me like a lioness protects her cubs! I am angry at Mommy for a lot of reasons. I am not going to totally confront her, because she is much older now and has changed. She has grown to be a nice lady.'

'Yes, I don't want to bother her with stories she can't remember even though it is because of all her blackouts when drinking and drugging and pure meanness, but I will continue with very little contact with her,' my dominant parent hand said.

'How many times did I have to come to a bar and escort her home, because she was drunk. I had to walk her home from the neighborhood bar behind the Safeway grocery store. She was stumbling and fell in the bushes. I just left her there. What could I do? I was only 11 years old. Then there was the bar by the TG&Y and I had to drive her home my non-dominant inner child hand wrote.

My right hand responded, "And at 18, I had to drive her to the hospital when she tried to commit suicide. She spent all her money on drugs, alcohol and cigarettes. I wonder, are my relatives at the family reunion all going to give me the silent treatment like they did when I decided to not talk to her the first time?'

I didn't let her know my address when I moved. I didn't tell her not telling where I worked. I didn't give her my email address or phone number. I never befriended her on Facebook and am very happy and relieved about it. I have my own space. I am free now.

So, this is my reality which clashes with my mother's, Mechthild of Magdeburg, a Medieval mystic said, "A fish cannot drown in water. A bird does not fall in air. Each creature God made must live in its own true nature." I live in my own true nature now which is my reality as I perceive it. I live and breathe healing from the abuse and through this book, I help others to heal and am now celebrating my life and experiences. I live naturally in my very own truth of what I perceived to have happened, not what my mother says happened.

I finally accepted the fact that mom didn't protect me. The kidnapping happened. The rapes by my father and grandfather happened. I realized I couldn't believe that my mother didn't protect me the way a lioness would protect her cub. She had no maternal instinct. She made no move to stop anyone from hurting me

ISA

I joined I.S.A., Incest Survivors Anonymous, and attended

their Long Beach, California meetings every Saturday. There were a

lot of good men and women there and through their camaraderie and

sharing, I learned and healed a great deal. I also benefitted from a

book called Courage to Heal by Ellen Bass and Laura Davis. I occasionally visited A.C.A., Adult Children of Alcoholics, which was helpful and my therapist had been sexually abused as well. Along with a therapist, it is a very good idea to see a doctor of psychiatry. Don't let their rates scare you. Many doctors have reduced rates for people with low incomes. I regret not getting on medication sooner.

The meetings and readings still transformed me. I studied the Twelve Steps with I.S.A. and finished a workbook with a small group of A.C.A. members. That helped me even though I was depressed, felt alienated from God, like an imposter at work and was very alone. I accepted my problems for the first time in my life and felt more free to be me. I wrote in my journal and studied my problems and reclaimed the little girl I had forgotten. Sure, she had been hurt a great deal, but also I remembered her sunny smile and playfulness. I stopped getting angry at my co-workers and transferred the anger to my parents where it rightfully belonged. I smiled more often, felt more calm around others, made friends more easily and became playful like the little girl inside me. I don't mean I was pregnant with a girl; I mean I saw a younger me in my mind.

I looked at the world a whole new way. It was like a fresh new day after a big rain. I could take on anything that came my way, because I now had the tools. Searching for truth is not living in the past, Psalm 18:28 promises, "The Lord my God will enlighten my darkness." Reading scriptures, survivors' biographies and journaling is searching for truth and recounting the flashes of memories that trigger. Remain open. There is something much bigger than you know going on here. I think one thing is for sure: maturity, grace and poise doesn't happen until you meet your past, and see it for what it is, deal with it and accept it.

Iyanla Vanzant states in Truth Postulate Number 5 of her book, One Day My Soul Just Opened Up, "There is a Divine Order to everything in life. It is for this reason that exactly where you are at any given time in life is exactly where you should be according to the Divine unfolding of your consciousness and life."

Fred and Florence Littauer in, Healing from Memories That Bind, tell us that "Awareness is the first step to freedom, and then the Lord can begin His restoration process." They also showed that 1 John 1:9 is operative in this situation, 'If we confess (acknowledge) our sins and those sins that were committed against us, he is faithful to forgive us of the guilt we often feel and cleanse us from the unrighteousness done to us.' How can we acknowledge a sin committed against us if we have no awareness of it?" The guilt you feel could arise from your belief that you deserved the abuse. That your young thin body was too attractive and this caused the sexual abuse.

So, first you cry. Then you get angry. It seemed the anger would never go away. I asked myself, what do I get if I let go of my anger? Then I caught a glimpse of the hurt little girl inside me. I thought that taking care of her was better than being angry. I experienced a shift and began to deal with my pain. Anger is a mask for hidden pain. I momentarily thought of suicide, but decided to stick around and live my life for the little girl inside me. Besides, she did nothing to deserve all this. She needed me to protect her against further harm. I met the challenge head on and didn't drink alcohol for two years.

After the breakthrough I soon turned 26 and worked at a stock brokerage firm. I gained the respect of my colleagues and became a good team worker. I generated more bon fide leads for the mutual fund salesmen than anyone else. Month after month I won a free lunch with the V.P. of Sales and sometimes the President of the company was there. My career was looking really good. But one day I was feeling a little too comfortable and told one of my co-workers the story about my kidnapping. I felt so alone and alien to everyone else, even though I already was well liked. I told the story and felt better afterwards. But to my demise he told the salesmen about it and rumors spread like wildfire. I felt naked, like they could see right through me. I had nowhere to hide.

I had a breakdown and wound up in the State Hospital for two weeks. The psychiatrist there tried to convince me that I had paranoid schizophrenia. I would not accept the diagnosis and when I got out, I did not take my medication, even thought I had accepted another job at a different securities brokerage firm. Because I didn't take my medication, I became sick again. My ex-boyfriend drove me from Southern California to Dallas, Texas so I could stay with my Aunt Rhonda and Uncle Ron.

I improved at my Aunt and Uncle's place and found a job at another brokerage firm. I was laid off and received a nice severance. I immediately got a job at a nice gift store making minimum wage. This whole time I was living with my Aunt and Uncle.

One day after work, I found myself driving all over Dallas. I can usually orient myself well, but this time I got very lost. I began hearing voices. I saw a red checkered water tower and thought I was in Sallisaw, Oklahoma where a Ralston store used to be. Their logo was a red checkered square on all their dog food packages. However, I was really in Carrollton Texas standing in the middle of the highway median talking to myself!

A patrolmen stopped and handcuffed me and took me to Parkland Hospital where I stayed a month to get diagnosed. This time, I believed the diagnosis of paranoid schizophrenia. My doctor said I was a highly operative schizophrenic. I knew those crazy thoughts in my head and the voices couldn't be real. At least I could accept that and realized what was wrong with me. It turned out that my little chemical imbalance could easily be treated with mild medication. Some people, bless their hearts, still hear voices and delusions even on medication. The stress of confronting reality caused the schizophrenia, which was a chance to live another reality because this one was unbearable.

I came home from the hospital and lived with my mom and stepfather for several months. I needed to trust my mother again, since she forsook me. I was afraid that if I didn't get my mother's love, I would wind up in a coma or be committed. She and I met at karaoke twice a week for 13 years and talked on the phone almost every day. Even though she never acknowledged the truth nor said she was sorry, I felt her love me as much as she could. She was finally gentle with me, instead of being angry and yelling at me all the time. This time healed the sad memories of when she abandoned me at 4 years old in the empty house.

I got a job at a place like Denny's and kept moving up until I was a fine dining waitress at a very nice seafood restaurant. That's where I met my future husband. He was a handsome auburn haired man at thirty-nine and I was thirty-four   He spent his years so far as a fine dining waiter, chef, bartender and limousine driver. We moved in together. He would collect the flowers from the restaurant table vases and surprise me by putting them in my bath water. My stepfather said my personality blossomed after I met Kevin. The only argument we had was who gets to cook dinner, until he learned that I was a pretty good cook. The first meal I cooked for him was mom's ex-boyfriend, Charlie's recipe      that he taught me. It was Fettuccini Alfredo with spicy Italian Sausage and sautéed onions and red bell pepper. He loved it! It is a very unique dish that you can't find in an Italian restaurant. Usually they just boil the sausage and don't brown it. Browning the sausage makes the dish look gorgeous and more appetizing.

One night I felt compelled to tell him the story about the kidnapping. At that point, I still hadn't remembered how I got home in the story. I hadn't remembered yet that I came home pregnant and my mother did not want me. I am sure deep inside of me, it was still too painful to remember. I asked Kevin what he thought about my story. I told him I still wasn't sure it really happened. He said, "Maybe it happened in another life." I cried, because I thought it was a blessing that he wasn't turned off by the story. That seemed like the perfect thing for him to say. He accepted the fact that I had schizophrenia and I felt his love for me.

We got married nine months later. We accept each other the way the we are. He never calls me slow and uncool like my brother and mom did. We had a lot in common and one of our vows is that we share our dream of living in a little log cabin in the woods. We're still working on that, but we have a beautiful home now and entertain our friends every Saturday night.

He has never asked me to go to work. However, he was so tired of the restaurant business and wanted to become a deck, fence and furniture builder. I got a job at a second hand bookstore to help make the transition and to help buy tools. It was there that I learned how to sell on Ebay. I have done real well selling valuable first edition books and now exercise equipment on Ebay, which gives me nice easy part time money. I have been selling on Ebay for 11 years and Kevin and sold 13 cars on it. He also has his thriving carpentry business that employs four men and one woman.

We have a lot in common and we love to camp. Our favorite place is Beaver's Bend, Oklahoma on the river. Occasionally we go to a bed and breakfast.

One important thing that keeps me grounded and assured of his love is a boxful of little notes about Kevin. People with schizophrenia need a lot of reassurance that they are loved. Every now and then I feel insecure and I open the box and read all the sweet loving things he has done that shows how much he cares for me. Like 'Kevin said he wants to fall asleep on the couch instead of the bedroom because I was in the living room not the bedroom,' or "Kevin took me to the country to take pictures of me kneeling in the beautiful Texas Bluebonnets." I have been collecting these notes for 5 years.

I got well from the memories of my dad, by talking a lot about it with my therapist. I also mourned over the fact that I really didn't have a decent father anyway. When he was dying of cancer, I didn't contact him or visit him in the hospice. He did not call me to ask why. I didn't go to his funeral. You can forgive but you don't have to forget and carry on a relationship with anyone.

My marriage is what healed me. My husband is in a way, a father figure that stands up to my need of respectability from him. He is a hard worker. He is kind and thoughtful, gentle and loving as well as very lovable.

I got the idea for the notes and boxes when I was talking to my therapist and said I sometimes questioned my husband's love for me and needed reassurance. She said, "Every time he shows you he loves you write it down on an index card and put it in a box. Then when you feel insecure, you can read all of them and that will change your feelings about your relationship and his love for you. I started doing this and now I am on my second box. You can read the notes listed in the appendix in the back.

About 4 or 5 years into our marriage, I realized I had a bad cycle of communication with my mother. I remembered more and more about her neglect and how she did not protect me from my dad. How she never called the police and continued to let him have joint custody of me every summer after their divorce. I began to recognize a vicious cycle between us. I was a housewife and had no children so I had plenty of time to ponder. I realized that she didn't really care about me. I harbored so much anger at her until I would pick up the phone to call her to hear her happy voice. Then I would feel relief because the phone call would make me think the opposite-that she did love me. On the one hand I thought Mom loved me and on the other hand I thought she didn't.

I realized that we only had certain things we could talk about without upsetting her. We could only talk about superficial things like clothes, food, karaoke, husbands, friends, the weather. She did not want to hear me share that I needed a good father while growing up. I needed a father to tell me about boys. I held onto my anger at my mother to keep from being angry at other people. My

Mom was drunk so much of the time and Dad wasn't there. My brother and I raised ourselves. We were basically orphans with a "zombie adult" in our home.

Mom divorced dad when I was three and dated one married man for 15 years and a second married man for 4 years. During that time whenever I brought it up that I needed a decent father to raise me, she would say in a deep mean voice, "Jeana, DON'T DO THIS!" I could not bring up the fact that she did not protect me from my dad and grandfather. It hurt to talk about it, because I knew she would deny ever knowing about it. Then I quit sitting at her table at karaoke. Soon, I quit saying goodbye to her when the karaoke evening was over. I would just leave and say goodbye to my friends without saying a word to her. She knew something was wrong.

We moved and I sent her an email that said I did not want to keep in touch with her because there are only a few things we can talk about. When I talked about things that really mattered to me she would get mad. She said in her email reply that my message took her breath away and that she always supported me. My mother is very unaware of herself.

One day when mom still had my phone number she called the day before Thanksgiving and ruin the big day I had planned. I got angry and hurt, so I put on my favorite CD, Gregorian Chants, side 1. She wanted to know if everything was okay. (Her guilt was getting to her). I answered that everything's fine. It really bothered me that none of my relatives would talk to me at the family reunion, because I wasn't talking to mom. Even Uncle Ron, who always said, 'it's none of his business', wasn't talking to me.

My mother's family followed each other like a herd of cattle and pointed fingers at others instead of at themselves. They tell you none of this is their business even though they are taking sides by not talking to me.

Later, I told mom about this and she said, "I don't remember" and "I'm sorry you feel that way." She never remembered anything and then always said, "I'm sorry you feel this way." and "I'm sorry IF that happened." I know it happened and I told her many times it happened. She should say, "I'm sorry I didn't protect you." NOT "I'm sorry IF I didn't protect you." She placed all the guilt, anger and hurt on me so she could rest easier on Thanksgiving.

After Thanksgiving I changed my telephone number and email address so there could be no contact. But she did know my home address and wrote me a short note requesting the phone number and email address. I responded, "At this time, in order for me to continue healing, I must decline." She has not contacted me since. I regained some peace of mind. I had to do it, because I found that I was still angry with her. When I cut off the communication, the anger lightened. I used to have a terrible time of gritting my teeth in my sleep and had to wear a mouth guard. I no longer grit my teeth. I like it this way. I quit hoping that my mother would own up to her responsibilities and apologize. I have moved on.

I still don't talk to her. I changed my phone number. Healing takes a lot of time and can come over a span of years, even decades. It also comes in phases or waves. Even though I healed a great deal, I still had to come to terms with my relationship with my Mother.

Unresolved anger is a block to our emotional growth. I have anger and repressed anger. Depression is repressed anger. Harnessing it into a productive force in my life will assist my emotional growth, like writing this book. It used to be that the thoughts were intrusive and left a feeling of superiority over those that did me wrong.

When we were engaged, I started having anxiety about the traditional father and bride dance. I started having creepy thoughts about him, that I hadn't had for 10 years. Back then, I realized my father had raped me when I was 13. I found it so disgusting and sad that I blocked it out of my mind and started having memories about the kidnapping instead.

I got well from the memories of my dad, by talking a lot about it with my therapist. I also mourned over the fact that I really didn't have a decent father in any way. When he was dying of cancer, I didn't contact him or visit him in the hospice. He did not call me to ask why. I didn't go to his funeral. You can forgive but you don't have to continue the relationship.

My marriage is what healed me. Now I take better care of myself. I walk Monday through Friday. I do yoga and foot baths and pedicures. I take more pride in my appearance and take better care of myself. My husband and I bought a beautiful used jacuzzi that I get into almost every day if the outside temperature is 50 degrees or more. I write in my journal which helps me write this book. I read inspirational books and listen to classic rock. Counseling and losing weight has given me a great deal of confidence. So much so that now I can say, "I am a child sexual abuse survivor." with my head held high instead of being embarrassed. When you heal yourself you will finally be able to tell about your past coming from a sense of strength instead of fear embarrassment and pain.

I have come to terms with my father and grandfather. They were immature and made poor life-choices. I believe Mom never called the police because she was afraid they'd discover that she was a drug addict and that she was conducting other illicit acts.

Hope and Forgiveness

*Faith is the substance of things hoped for, evidence of things not*

*seen.* (Hebrews 11:1-2).

I have hope because I have a sense of purpose for my life.

For instance, I am passionate about this book, healing myself and

helping others heal. I hope they will draw inspiration from this

victory over my traumas. If you don't have a purpose then you

can't have hope. Your purpose could be weeding the garden. The

result could be that someone looks for your flowerbed every time

they drive by your home and the beauty of it uplifts them. I would like to do that one day but for now I have books to write! At first my purpose was to find love for the woman I was and to take my little girl inside along with me. I believe I have the ability to heal now and completely in the future. I believe that I will live a very long life and will have completely healed. The pain of my child within is still being healed in layers, years later.

I heal my child within by drinking Chamomile tea out of a teddy bear cup. This tea has a very calming effect and is the tea Peter Rabbit drank. I have been sleeping with a stuffed animal since I was 26 and am now 49 and have been married for almost 14 years. I stopped sleeping with the teddy bear for a short time after I was married and then my husband surprised me with another bear to sleep with and he didn't mind my sleeping with it. I retired my 'little girls' teddy bear. After almost 13 years of not sleeping with it, I put my child's teddy next to me on the pillow. That night I had a vivid dream of being a Snow Queen. I saw a gold, silver and blue steeple with pink party favors. Then I was transported to the top of the steeple and it rose upward into a blue sky with snowflakes, diamonds and stars that twirled around and round me. I believe the dream was a gift from my little girl, because I brought the bear back to her. I sleep with two Teddy Bears now on the bed but not in my arms. Sometimes I hold onto a paw.

I draw pictures of things I don't intellectually understand. I had flashes of a room in my grandparents home and could not make anything of it. I drew a picture of it with crayons and came to terms with my grandpa's incessant and violent sexual abuse.

I have patience when it comes to healing because it takes time and comes in layers. Abuse comes in layers over time and so healing comes in layers also. Others may expect you to be healed but they are wrong. Don't quit before your miracles. Don't quit your healing process by sliding back into your addictions. God protects you to keep you from remembering until God reveals. Then he will help you heal your memories.

Forgiveness comes from being able to see the offender as a victim, because he or she is still in darkness and you have come out of the darkness. It is rare that the perpetrator will not own 100% or even 50% of the responsibility for the abuse. Often, they think they are teaching the child about sex and are proud of it even if it becomes violent. So, If you accuse them of rape they will say they never raped the child.

You may not heal in a few years because we are made up of three things just like an egg. In the innermost part, there is your spirit and God which is the yolk. Surrounding that center is the soul which is made up of mind, will and emotions. The soul is the largest part of the egg. And the third and last component is the shell which is your body. This is made up of bruises, broken bones and body memories. You heal in these layers. If your spirit isn't healed, you won't be able to heal your soul and body. Your soul is the things you love like music. Your spirit is your special gifts God gave you. Healing my spirit is my main priority. I fulfill this by reading inspirational books, doing yoga and listening to spiritual music such as Gregorian Chants. When I feel especially good, I listen to 70s rock and roll which is all the time! I love listening to music more than watching TV. I love a really good rock and roll concert DVD. I am a Garden Club member, and hostess parties for friends and have returned to going to karaoke.

The mind is composed of thoughts, memories and decisions. You cannot have hope without faith. You use free will in your soul to choose to heal your spirit. God wants you to have your free will to forgive and see your perpetrators as victims. He may not totally heal you and erase all memories and pain, because that is how he keeps you tethered to his side. He loves you. You are unique. You have discovered your authentic self, so take care of it. Abuse distorts the soul's perspectives. What about those who refuse to admit that they did this to you. The offender who hurt you is an even bigger victim. Those who hurt are hurting.

Courage to pursue healing without knowing what lies ahead is faith. Especially if you have memories you have not yet uncovered. Persist in the healing process even if it hurts. It is like learning to ride a bike. You fall off, it hurts and you get back on the bike. You will never forget how to ride a bike and once you have started to heal yourself you will never forget how.

Our group in the Healing Hearts Ministries are women and men that work on their domestic violence and sexual assault issues. Dona said, "when you forgive you regain your power." Chrissy and Mary say prayers for their abuser for God to save his or her soul.

One aspect of your spiritual journey is forgiveness of self, forgiveness of others and forgiveness of God. Can I forgive my mother the time she walked in on my dad sexually abusing me and she walked out of the room without helping me? My Mother made me feel shame and doubt in my cognitive ability. She didn't apologize which made me feel like all this was in my mind. She only called to keep tabs on me and monitor me. She didn't care about my reality or my beliefs. It is as if her reality was valid and mine was my imagination. That is abuse, also..

I forgave God first because Jesus forgave him and me. Healing Hearts Ministries tells us, "Problems are merely wrapped in possibilities and potential, waiting for wings. You have problems in the cocoon until you get wings and become a butterfly. The problem is how to get out of the cocoon." Its like how to unlock your mind as if it were a Rubic's cube and find your soul and spirit.

The day I found Healing Hearts Ministries and all the special women and men in it was when I broke out of the cocoon and got my wings to heal again. They gave me the courage to have unyielding confidence.

Actor, Jake Gyllenhaal said, "When something tears your heart out of a situation, you never know where the heart will find itself again." I compare this statement to the family I had then and the family I have now.

You will know when forgiveness has begun when you recall those who hurt you and feel the power to wish them well. (Lewis B. Smedes). When I was twenty-five, I began telling my Mom about my pain and internal torment. I told her I needed her to read <u>Healing The Child Within,</u> because it would help her understand why and how I hurt. I am now 50 years old and she has yet to read it.

I forgave her for her treatment of me. However, I don't have to carry on a relationship with her and be continually reminded of my past. She is a nice lady now so I don't want to bother her with my anger. I believe this is sowing a spirit of forgiveness and mercy, because I handle her with compassion.

Mercy does not expose other people's faults. Mercy doesn't judge. We can judge the sin, but not the person, because we don't know their story about what has happened in their lives that causes them to hurt us. *Mercy over judgement. James 2:13.* In order to get past the abuse, I had to forgive my mother and others who didn't help me.

After cutting off ties with her four years ago, I have come to believe that breaking off ties with her is totally acceptable. Cutting off ties with her protects my inner child that was neglected and hurt over and over again.

Now I am not alone or have to be on the defensive all the time. It's a shiny new day after a big rain. Now I know, thanks to Mertie, that God resides inside. And thanks to Dr. Whitfield, author of <u>Healing the Child Within</u>, I know I have a child within. What this means to me is that God is within me and has been all my life because I have seen Him in my mind and spirit in all my past. I can see God in the memory of my smile and bright eyes while looking at Mertie as a child.

God's spirit is playful as a child. God gives others confidence, intelligence, soft and strong at the same time, and his light never goes out. Nobody can take God from you because he is always inside so you can share Him.

Never close the door on your past. Tether it to your side the way God tethers you to His side.

My Lilac Room

*The truth will set you free.*

I like writing in my journal in the middle of the night in my guest bedroom. My favorite inspirational music is a Gregorian Chants CD. It is made up of songs sung by monks in a Scottish Abbey. The candelabra on my writing desk has five pink coach candles lit.

I am sitting on a stool that goes with my 1920s vanity and desk. I sewed the pink skirt on the desk and bought a glass topper to protect it. It matches the lilac walls. The brushed metal bed is full size with a white Battenberg lace duvet covering a goose down comforter. And a beautiful brown almost black velvet pillow lies on the bed. Two European sized pillows covered in lilac damask was a splurge.

A quilt stand has a small pink embroidered quilt that matches the walls perfectly. I am burning lavender incense and drinking ice cold Pepsi One's with a cuzzy. There is a small patchwork quilt with pink gingham and roses at the foot of the bed. This is my sanctuary and I use this room to write in my journal and read inspirational books in order to heal myself from the pain in my heart. Beautiful!

I am reading Iyanla Vanzant's <u>One Day My Soul Just Opened Up</u>. It is full of her beliefs she has about God, spirituality and herself. One of the most interesting passages about prayer is this, "What we pray for we already have; but in most cases, we are not aware of it. Prayer is actually an affirmation of what already exists. Call forth the Divine not because you don't know what to do but because you know what to do and need strength to do it."

She also wrote, "Anything you need to know, you will know. You will be instructed if there is anything you need to do. You may see or hear something. You may not." And "Love will heal anything that is not an expression of love." And I say this: If you are angry about the harm others have done to you, then self-love will heal you. How you treat yourself determines how others will treat you now and in the future. (Self-love will increase your self-esteem and how you feel about yourself). What is self-love? Saying no occasionally. Giving yourself a pedicure. Eating and drinking good food. Using portion control when eating and doing yoga.

The counseling of HHM in Terrell, Texas has given me a great deal of confidence. So much so that now I can say, "I am a child sexual abuse survivor." with my head held high. The perpetrators never want us to talk about it to protect themselves and for us to be quiet in our deep shame.

**THE TRUTH WILL SET YOU FREE**

# BIBLIOGRAPY

Whitfield M.D., Charles L. *Healing the Child Within, Discovery and Recovery for Adult Children of Dysfunctional Families.* Deerfield Beach, Florida: Health Communications, Inc., 1987.

Today's English Version. *Good News Bible.* Nashville, Tennessee: Thomas Nelson Publishers, 1986.

Vanzant, Iyanla. *One Day My Soul Just Opened Up.* New York: Simon & Schuster, 1998.

Littauer, Fred & Florence. *Freeing Your Mind From Memories That Bind, How to Heal the Hurts of the Past.* San Bernardino, California: Here's Life Publishers, 1988.

# APPENDIX

Here is what the notes say:

Before we moved from Dallas to a town north of there, I got
cranky one day. So, he drove us a long way to our soon to be
new home, the sea foam green colored 900 sq.ft. trailer. He
showed me a beautiful sunset going down over our expansive
wildflower meadow adjacent to our backyard. There were three
horses and my favorite, a donkey. Isn't that sweet?

He surprised me by taking me to see my favorite FoodTV
network chef, Jamie Oliver. He was at the Central Market
grocery store putting on a cooking show.          I was so excited,
I got tears in my eyes.

He stays with me even though I go through periods of time when
I am overweight.

When I got mentally sick in Yantis, Texas out in the countryside
there was no room at the hospital after 911 happened. We
realized I wouldn't get the care I needed. We had to move back
to Dallas even though we had just bought a doublewide mobile
home. We couldn't sell it and lost $25,000.00 on the deal, but he
never said a word about it.

I was crying because I didn't think he was attracted to me
anymore. He said, "I want to love you and make love to you for

the rest of our lives."

He comes home early to have more time with me!

He is very patient with me, especially when I forget things or ask him to repeat what he is saying.

He was driving by the record store and thought of me. He stopped and bought me Alana Myles record 'Black Velvet' so I could practice the song for karaoke. That was very thoughtful of him.

He came over to help me babysit until midnight. I thought that was really nice.

I had my hair in a ponytail and he said I looked 5 years younger.

He surprised me when he set up a workshop for me in our dining room. He placed a very large board over the table for a work space and lined up paint cans behind it. I arranged silk flowers behind cottage style windows on the table.

When I was pregnant, he would come home as I was sleeping and kiss me saying, 'I love you so much.'

My husband likes to camp with just the two of us.

I broke my toe, but I could still walk. He went out and bought tape and bandages anyway.

I told Kevin I was afraid of becoming old and unable to tweeze the dark hairs on my chin. 'I would hate for you to see me like that.' He said he would tweeze them for me. Isn't that nice? That's love.

I remember Kevin always going to my psychiatrist appointments with me and we picked up my subscriptions together, even in the dead of winter.

He washes and vacuums my truck regularly.

Kevin took pictures of me among the flowers at the Tyler Rose Garden.

He likes to hug me.

When he got his Christmas bonus, he bought us a dinner with steak, lobster and crab instead of something for himself.

Kevin takes a nap in the living room, because that was where I am.

When we watch TV on the couch he sometimes rests his hand on the center of my back.  It is very loving and healing.

When I came home from the hospital, after getting well from pneumonia, I found he had cleaned the house, bought me flowers and cooked dinner.

When I feel insecure about his love for me I can read these notes and then I feel much better.

I am very fortunate to be loved by such a nice man
My husband is old school.  He has never asked me to get a job, even though he works really hard in the heat and cold building decks and fences.

He stayed up in the hospital room all night when I broke my wrist.
He buys me flowers just because.

My husband and I stayed together the whole day around our fire on the first day of Fall.  No TV!

Kevin had to get an EKG, blood test, and stool sample done for a prostate exam.  He told me that if anything happened to him unexpectedly that he wanted to make sure I didn't think he didn't love me.  So he hugged me and we said we loved each other and kissed.

I am not 2nd best.  I am number 1 with him.

He is a great lover.

We had a nice Valentine's Day dinner at The Forge in Ben Wheeler, TX and stayed in a cabin.  At dinner he said we should renew our wedding vows in the old little church there, and I cried happy tears.  That night we cuddled in bed.

My husband said he is totally happy and would never leave me.

We have been married 14 years.

He worked on Saturday chopping down a tree.  That night he took me to my favorite restaurant.  At dinner he said he will always work extra jobs so we can do special things like this.

Early in our marriage he said, "What do I have to do to get you to know I love you?  Jump out in front of a car on the freeway?"

He drives me to appointments all over Dallas-Ft.Worth area and East Texas.  We pick up gym equipment I find in the classifieds. He wants me to be protected and safe.  I have been selling the gym equipment on Ebay for 7 years.

It was his idea to take me to Heart and Sheryl Crow concerts, my favorite bands!

Kevin said, "There isn't anyone else he'd rather make love to than me."

He took some time off near Christmas.  Wednesday through Saturday night he spent with me and nobody else.  He didn't work on trucks with his buddies.  It was really nice.  Then we drove around to look at Christmas lights.  It was his idea!

He has nightmares that he is losing me or can't get to me and wakes up very upset.

He bought me incense and made me two large incense holders for the long stick kind.

My husband said, "There are two things I promised myself: 1) Never marry. 2) Never divorce. I broke the first promise, but I will never get a divorce." That made me feel good, loved and secure.

He said he loves me more than anything in the whole world.

He put bright colorful Gerber daisies in my bath water.

Our friend Val said, "He tells me all the time how much he loves you."

He said he is not going anywhere. He will only marry once and does not believe in secrets from each other including infidelity.

He quit drinking when I quit to be in solidarity with me.

When we were dating he said he wanted to do more things with me than just going out for drinks. Like going to the Butterfly Botanical Garden, museums and movies and picnics.

He said, "Younger women are stupid."

The day before Valentine's Day he bought me beautiful pink roses that opened up wide into big floppy flowers. They lasted for a week and a half.

We get each other early gifts before birthdays, Valentine's Day, Anniversaries and Christmas because we can't wait to see each others' smiles and happy eyes when we open the gift.

Made in the USA
Middletown, DE
14 June 2023

32567537R00066